A Gravedigger's Churchyard Tales

By

Ian Shipley

Grosvenor House
Publishing Limited

This book is published by
Grosvenor House Publishing Ltd
Link House
140 The Broadway, Tolworth, Surrey, KT6 7HT.
www.grosvenorhousepublishing.co.uk

A CIP record for this book
is available from the British Library

ISBN 978-1-80381-604-3

With thanks to:

Boz Mugabe (Artwork)

Nick Jones (Full Proof)

Paul Shipley

David Shipley

Gary Jones

Johnathon ?

Ben Burgess

Neil Alexander

Kieran Barraclough

William Dunn

Paul Foster

Stephen Edwards

Neil Grebbie

David Longden

Contents

Chapter 1	The Lincoln Edge	1
Chapter 2	Three Polish Airmen	5
Chapter 3	Our Ever-Changing World	9
Chapter 4	Bleak House Murder	14
Chapter 5	Back-Breaking Day	17
Chapter 6	Farewell Newark Cemetery	20
Chapter 7	You've Dug It Wrong	24
Chapter 8	Stone on the Hill	26
Chapter 9	Always Expect the Unexpected	28
Chapter 10	One Grumpy Vicar	31
Chapter 11	I Won't Get Fooled Again	34
Chapter 12	All Saints Churchyard, Eagle	37
Chapter 13	Plot 15H	40
Chapter 14	Is Everything Alright?	44
Chapter 15	Stuck in the Mud	48
Chapter 16	My Close Encounter with Death	51
Chapter 17	Grafting in a Downpour	55
Chapter 18	Beware the Rare Tall Thrift Plant	58

Chapter 19	The Old Rectory Courtyard	61
Chapter 20	When Death Comes to Call	63
Chapter 21	One of Those Days	66
Chapter 22	An Open-Cast Mine	68
Chapter 23	Never Be Complacent	71
Chapter 24	Eight Days a Week	73
Chapter 25	Hill Top Cemetery, Gonerby	76
Chapter 26	You Got Deeper than the Last Gravedigger	79
Chapter 27	Whoops, I Pegged Out the Wrong Grave	82
Chapter 28	Graveside Catastrophe	84
Chapter 29	Newark Castle Ghost Hunt	87
Chapter 30	Postponed Until Further Notice	90
Chapter 31	Thank You, Mr Jackson	92
Chapter 32	It's Time to Share the Workload	95
Chapter 33	Don't Go to Syerston	98
Chapter 34	Who Put That There?	100
Chapter 35	The Covid Pandemic	103
Chapter 36	Graveyard Antics	105
Chapter 37	A 34-Year Secret	113

CHAPTER 1

The Lincoln Edge

The Edge – or the Lincoln Cliff, as it is also known – is a prominent prehistoric escarpment, which rises 200 feet above the Trent Valley.

Gravedigging in the churchyards and cemeteries along this forbidding track is vastly different to its neighbouring county, Nottinghamshire. A combination of sandstone, limestone, clay and marl, the Edge is enough to test the patience of any hand-digging gravedigger.

For years I had been fortunate, as the majority of my work had been completed within the ease of the Trent Valley, but as time progressed I was to find myself ever more in demand, and my growing workload began taking me to the villages along the Lincolnshire Edge.

Gravedigging is exacting work, often taking many hours to complete. Colleagues often asked: 'Why don't you buy yourself a machine and save yourself all that grief?'

I've never had the desire to buy a machine, though in recent years I have replaced my worn-out pickaxe with a jackhammer.

I'm a stickler for a neat, traditionally shaped grave, and so I'd much prefer to toil to the point of exhaustion rather than be sat on my backside pulling a few levers, which, yes, would make my job easier, but would give me no satisfaction at all.

Besides, I've always stated that if those before me could hand-dig graves, then I can see no reason why it cannot be done today. With time and patience they are doable, though up on the Edge, the majority are only dug to single depth. Bedrock and water are the main factors that make it difficult to get any deeper.

At first, I laboured unnecessarily as I strived to reach what I would consider to be an acceptable depth of between 48 and 54 inches.

When working in the churchyards, I would often chance upon a retired gravedigger who time and again would specify '40 to 43 inches. You'll get no more as the land will see to that.'

Crossing the border into unknown territory is all well and good, but there was an ever-increasing danger that at some point I would spread myself too thin. For a number of years, I had been blessed in the knowledge that if I needed backup assistance when work got busy, I could call on my brothers, Paul and Dave; my employee, Gary; and, occasionally, my wife, Alison.

During the particularly harsh winters of 2009 and 2010, the burial rate shot up twofold. With Paul recovering from a hernia operation and Dave entirely snowed in, the demanding workload pushed Gary and me to near exhaustion. Deep snow and untreated roads led to many hazardous trips, and with funeral directors unwilling to cancel any burials, it remained business as usual.

Unfortunately, it got so busy that I had no choice but to turn work down, as I could not physically do any more. It was frustrating, as work was work. Nevertheless, eleven burials in eight working days, in the depths of winter, was just too much.

As it turned out, there were two jobs I'm now glad I turned down.

The first, on the far side of Sleaford, was for the interment of a young lad who tragically had been killed over the Christmas holidays. As I could not help, the funeral director passed the work to a colleague.

Unfortunately, adding to the family's heartache, my colleague was given the wrong coffin size, and as a result it did not fit the grave.

In addition, I received a telephone call from an undertaker who expressed that he was in desperate need of my services. It was 4 p.m. on a dark winter's afternoon. He explained that he had a burial at Waddington Cemetery for noon the next day and that he'd forgotten to book a gravedigger. I didn't get the chance to explain that I could not help due to other commitments, as when I said I couldn't do it, the grouchy undertaker promptly hung up. Needless to say, from that day to this I have not received any further work from him.

That night, Waddington airfield, which backs on to the cemetery, recorded a temperature of minus 13.5 degrees.

Waddington can be a horrible dig at the best of times. It's all stone, and even with my trusty jackhammer there was no way I could have completed the work within such a tight deadline.

The two harsh winters had opened my eyes. I realised I could not physically be in three different village locations, on the same day, within hours of each other, especially when the weather was bad.

No job is worth making yourself ill over, and after hearing that a colleague had suffered a stroke, brought on by a heavy workload, I decided, as I did not want to end up the same way, to cut back, and thus I withdrew my services from my local surrounding area.

Nowadays, I do occasionally dig the odd grave along the Edge, but despite repeated requests, I have kept away from offering my services full-time.

CHAPTER 2

Three Polish Airmen

On a cold snowy day in November 2010, I undertook what turned out to be my last notable job at Newark Cemetery.

My task was the exhumation of three Polish army officers who'd died in the same plane crash that had killed their wartime leader, General Wladyslaw Sikorski.

Despite an inquiry ruling that the crash had been an accident, many believed there was more to it. There were suggestions that the accident was the work of Stalin's assassins or British agents working under Churchill's orders. There was even speculation that the three coffins of these officers might be empty.

The bodies to be exhumed were those of Major General Tadeusz Klimecki, Colonel Andrzej Marecki and Lieutenant Józef Ponikiewski.

Although I was working in conjunction with the council and a local funeral director, I was ill at ease at the thought of carrying out the work, as the initial instruction to complete the task quickly and professionally was for the most part left with me.

I had some knowledge of exhumations, but they weren't something I did regularly, and nor would I want to, as it is a complex task that can be beset by unforeseen difficulties.

Without doubt, this would be my most challenging job to date.

At 8.30 a.m. on Sunday 28 November 2010, I began a preliminary dig of the three graves in order to determine whether they had been a standard burial or placed in a constructed brick-built vault.

In many ways, I was not looking forward to them being a standard burial, as they would not only be difficult to remove, but would take longer to do. Thankfully, the fact-finding dig revealed that the interments had been placed inside three individual, single-depth vaults, which had been sealed with paving slabs. Under the slabs, in each vault, were metal reinforced strips that ran the length and breadth, thus strengthening the lid.

With care, one slab was removed from each grave. Favourably, the burial chambers were all water-free. However, in each vault, it was noticeable that the outer wooden coffins had perished. A closer inspection revealed that each airman's remains had primarily been sealed within a lead-lined coffin.

Additionally, each coffin was resting on brick plinths. This was helpful, as it would make their removal a bit easier.

9 a.m., Thursday 2 December 2010

Heavy snow blanketed the cemetery. The marquee was up, all three vaults were open and ready, health and safety equipment in place, walk-boards laid, generator and lights primed, everything was ready to go.

The exhumation began at 10 a.m. with approximately twenty-five people in attendance. The first coffin to be removed was that of Tadeusz Klimecki. Eight men lifted in what turned out to be a straightforward procedure. The coffin was placed to one side before being carefully opened. Once the lid had been removed, both I and my colleague and indeed all those around us assumed the worst – that the coffin was empty. At first glance, that seemed to be the case. On closer investigation, however, we located the remains of a body. Although the deceased had been wrapped in a standard army-issue blanket, you could see his military uniform beneath.

The remains were then transferred to a new coffin. When each body was removed from the site, a prayer was said, followed by a minute's silence. This was done for all three officers.

The second exhumation, that of Andrzej Merecki, was the most troublesome, as the coffin had filled with water. It was so heavy that we could not physically lift it out of the vault. Therefore, a decision was made to raise one end of the coffin before piercing holes in the underside, thus draining away the stomach-churning fluid. Nevertheless, despite our best efforts, eight men still laboured to remove it. When we opened it up, the remains were so decomposed that my colleague and I scooped them out using a shovel.

It was not a pleasant task.

The final coffin to be removed was that of Józef Ponikiewski.

Of the three, this one appeared to be more decomposed than the others, as most of the outer wooden box had disintegrated. However, looks can be deceiving, and once the webbings were looped around the coffin, it was removed with relative ease.

Again, it was placed to the side, opened, and the remains transferred to another coffin.

Despite the worry and loss of sleep, this had been a fascinating task, one that I was only too glad to have been a part of. Even so, I'm in no hurry to carry out another.

CHAPTER 3

Our Ever-Changing World

People often say to me, 'One thing's for certain: you'll never be out of work.'

There was a time when I would definitely have shared that opinion, but nowadays I'm not so sure, especially as burial is becoming less frequent.

Nearly all of the cemeteries I currently visit do seemingly have enough allocated burial space for the coming years, but the same cannot be said for the village churchyards.

Over the last few years, I have seen a significant decrease in the number of burials, specifically new burials. Over the past 41 years, I have dug on average approximately 114 graves per calendar year, though that number is slowly decreasing.

There are a wide range of factors that account for this. Nationally, on average only three out of every ten funerals are now burials, as more people are opting for cremation.

Furthermore, many village churchyards are almost full, and many do not have the means to extend, nor indeed the funds to purchase additional land. To help alleviate this problem, permission was recently granted for the reuse of unmarked graves that are 75 years old. This was once 100 years.

In addition, many local parishes have now introduced stringent policies that allow you to be buried in the churchyard only if you were born and bred locally, or if you have a valid connection to the village.

Obtaining suitable land for establishing new cemeteries is particularly difficult, as burial space is seen as hijacking prime house-building land. Maintenance of graves is costly. What's more, there are the environmental issues regarding the embalming of bodies and the use of formaldehyde and other chemicals, which may leak into the water table.

Cremation too is under scrutiny, as it is said to use large amounts of non-renewable energy. It also releases toxic gases into the air, including mercury from dental fillings.

I assume that as long as burial continues to remain a personal choice, then provision will be made for those who wish to be interred, and therefore the services of a gravedigger will be required.

What I find sad is that the sighting of the traditional gravedigger like me, who on a regular basis journeys from churchyard to churchyard, will become a thing of the past.

I believe there will always be a need for a gravedigger, but his workload within the local parishes will be minimal, and so there will not be enough burials to sustain a full-time position.

Touch wood, health permitting, I still have a few good years ahead of me. After that, who knows? I'd always planned to pass on my old-style skills, just as they were taught to me, but unfortunately today's generation are quick to turn their nose up at hard manual graft, and so unfortunately I may, in this area at least, be the last of the traditional, old-style gravediggers.

In the churchyards, burial plots will continue to be reserved for the lucky few, but as villages expand and younger generations move in, then I can see your only choice will be cremation, or, at double the fees, a burial at your nearest cemetery.

In 2007 an alternative to burial and cremation was introduced. It is known as resomation (and also as water cremation or aqua-cremation).

It is a process that uses water and alkaline to break down human tissue. This process is gaining popularity across Europe and is currently legal in 20 states in the US.

In what is called a resomator, the body is placed in a coffin or shroud which is made from biodegradable material. Inside this steel chamber, a mixture of 95 per cent water and 5 per cent alkaline is heated to a temperature of 160 degrees centigrade, which is slightly cooler than the cremation process.

The body dissolves in three to four hours, leaving just the skeletal remains, which are then crushed before being put into an urn. This process is said to produce a third less in greenhouse gases than a standard cremation.

The fluid that was used to decompose the body can then be given to farmers to fertilise their fields. There have been many trials regarding any environmental issues, but in 2019 it was deemed a safe process.

Is this the future? Most people will take some convincing, as they did when cremation was first introduced. Nevertheless, I can see that eventually the crematoriums will be replaced, and so resomation may become standard practice.

To be honest, I'm not sure how I'd feel about eating vegetables that had been fertilised by human bodies.

In 2011 a process dubbed promession or corpse composting was introduced in Sweden, whereby the body is frozen by immersion in liquid nitrogen to make it brittle. The frozen remains are then shattered by vibration. All metals are sieved out and the remaining powdered dust is placed into a biodegradable casket which is then buried. It is said that this degrades fully within a year.

I don't fancy either of the above options. Neither do I want to be cremated. I have chosen burial, and in 2017 I purchased my final resting place in the cemetery at Collingham.

I do hope that my grave can be hand-dug the traditional way, but I fear that there may be no one to do it!

If cremation became my only option, then I do like the idea of having my ashes put into a firework – a rocket – and launched high into the sky, thus dispersing my remains in a blaze of colour.

What a way to go.

CHAPTER 4

Bleak House Murder

Every now and again I'd be assigned a job that would repetitively play on my mind, and no job did this more than the burial of teenager Fred Barras.

On Saturday 21 August 1999, the body of Fred Barras, from Newark-on-Trent, Nottinghamshire, was found lying in undergrowth at the back of Bleak House Farm in Emneth, Norfolk. He had been shot and killed by farmer Tony Martin.

Across the country it made headlines and everybody was talking about it. The news story was the biggest to hit Newark since January 1992, when estate agent Stephanie Slater was kidnapped by murderer Michael Sams.

Despite digging many graves over the course of my career, I was more uneasy about doing this job than any other, as the shooting had provoked a lot of anger within the town. It had divided opinions too.

The actual date and time of the burial was made known only to those who needed to know. Furthermore, I had been asked not to prepare the grave until the very last minute. With this in mind, I did not begin digging until late afternoon on the day prior to the interment.

Regardless of this, snooping journalists soon arrived. They'd been lying in wait and hanging around the cemetery all day, and once they saw me with shovel in hand, they immediately enquired, 'Is this for Fred?'

My two colleagues and I had been warned about their interest and had been told that if they asked, we were to say nothing. In fact, all cemetery staff had been strictly instructed not to get into conversation with anyone.

The casket-shaped, double-depth grave proved difficult to dig, as the hot summer months had dried up the land. It was slow-going and I was beginning to feel the pressure, as I was trying to complete it quickly and quietly. Additionally, the family had requested that all the spoil be removed from site.

As it was a gruelling dig, I'd opted not to shore up the grave. This was probably my biggest worry, as the last thing I needed was for it to collapse while the mourners were stood graveside.

However, I was confident it would stand. Besides, I did not wish to be seen or photographed after the interment standing in the grave removing the shoring, as that would not look good.

Fred Barras was laid to rest in Newark Cemetery on 9 September 1999. By midday the town centre of

Newark was at a complete standstill as hundreds of mourners attended the service at Newark's parish church. From there, the procession slowly made its way to the cemetery. The young man's casket was both carried and lowered by the family themselves.

At the family's request, there was no police presence, and there were no prying telescopic lenses. In fact, apart from my colleagues and me and those attending the burial, the cemetery was completely deserted. Oddly, on the day there was an unnerving calmness, an eerie, unnatural silence that seemingly cloaked the cemetery. It was very strange!

Thankfully, much to everyone's relief, especially mine, the burial concluded without incident. Phew!

CHAPTER 5

Back-Breaking Day

11 May 2009. Two days prior to me digging at Washingborough churchyard in Lincolnshire, I had dug and prepared a grave at Newark Cemetery in readiness for what was expected to be a big gypsy funeral.

The grave was a pre-purchased family plot, double depth, casket shaped, adequately shored, and all spoil had been removed from site, meaning that all was ready to go.

Knowing that Washingborough would be a formidable challenge, I enlisted the help of a colleague, and with a scorcher of a day forecast, I decided to beat the blistering heat by starting extremely early.

Still, no matter how hard you try, these difficult sandstone digs cannot be hurried, even with a jackhammer. Fortunately, this was just single depth, but all the same, I was making slow progress as the stubborn stuff refused to dig out easily.

At just after 11 a.m., I received a phone call informing me that there was a problem with the grave I had dug in

Newark. It emerged that due to family status, the grave should not have been dug where it had been. It should have been positioned in the adjoining plot. The voice on the phone asked me to leave whatever else I was doing and quickly return in order to backfill the grave and dig another.

Understandably, I was slightly maddened at having to put in extra work, but even so I said, 'Yes, I should be finished at Washingborough by early afternoon, and then I'll come straight across and sort it out.'

The reply I got was somewhat unexpected and slightly unnecessary, as I was directly told: 'I think you're forgetting who you are contracted to, Ian. I'll be expecting to see you in due course.'

Red rag to a bull was that. Somewhat miffed at the council's outburst, I merely ignored their request and proceeded to finish what I was doing. I didn't arrive back at Newark Cemetery until mid-afternoon, but once on site I immediately got stuck into rectifying the job.

Because we'd removed all spoil from plot 4, it made sense for all spoil we removed from plot 3 to be thrown into the other open grave.

As the empty grave began to top up, I proceeded to remove the hydraulic shoring units. My intention was to refix them in the new grave. Unfortunately, Mother Nature had a different idea. As soon as the units were released, the dividing wall between the two graves collapsed. It was a right mess!

This left a gaping hole on one side. It took a bit of organising, but between us we managed to refix and safely shore up both sides, though it still left a vast open void at the top of the grave. This we covered with hefty walk-boards, ensuring there was at least a sturdy platform to stand on. That's all I could do.

Under the blazing sun, we had completed two digs and a 12-hour shift, and I for one was knackered!

On the day of the Newark burial, I had to return to Washingborough. This meant I had to leave the Newark job in the hands of my capable colleague.

Understandably, he was worried sick that it might all go pear-shaped, and that he would be to blame. There was little else I could do, as my colleague had also declined to take my van and hence exchange jobs.

By chance, my brother Dave was available, and so he saved the day by hurrying across from Derby to assist my displeased workmate. Morale was further restored when I managed to return to Newark just as the funeral ended, and so all was good.

As for the council – no thank you, no apology. And to think, I didn't even invoice them for a re-dig or for the employment of an extra man. Typical!

CHAPTER 6

Farewell Newark Cemetery

Saturday 19 March 2011 was a particularly sad day for me because after almost three decades, my residency as chief gravedigger at Newark's London Road Cemetery was at an end.

For a while there had been whispers that my current contract would not be renewed, and so when eventually I was officially told, it came as no surprise. All the same, it was hard to comprehend, as I had hoped that it was nothing more than hearsay. I was not ready to leave, especially as it was not of my choosing.

I had worked at Newark Cemetery for 29 years. In this one cemetery alone, I had dug over 3,000 graves. Now, my traditional working methods had been deemed out of date, and I was to be replaced by a machine.

My contract formally ended on 19 January 2011, but as the council had not yet put anything in place, I was asked if I'd continue digging graves there for a further two months. This I agreed to do, but believe me when I say that those interim few weeks were not easy.

To be honest, I had looked forward to an additional three-year deal, after which I had planned to wind down my remaining years by completing work in the surrounding villages.

It's a certainty that a three-year extension on my contract would have helped me to fulfil my personal goal of hand-digging 5,000 graves. With the extension, I would have reached this milestone back in 2022, which also happened to be when I marked 40 years in the business.

As it is, if health permits, I will now have to endure another four years of hard toil to hit my goal.

My time at Newark had for the most part been fulfilling. I'm grateful to the old-timers who taught me a trade which has kept me in regular work, and chocolate biscuits, for over four decades.

Despite being promoted to cemetery foreman (1997 to 2003), my only failure, if indeed it can be called one, was that I did not make cemetery superintendent, a role that I would have undertaken with equal commitment.

My final dig at Newark Cemetery was on 14 March 2011. Assisted by long-term friend and colleague Gary Jones, I dug out a seven-foot-six – that is, treble-depth – grave. The day was doubly sad, because without this contract I could no longer employ Gary, which itself was a hard decision to swallow.

After completing my last backfill, I said my goodbyes and off I quietly went. I wasn't unduly upset, because for over a decade I had, independently of Newark, been labouring my wares around the villages of Lincolnshire and Nottinghamshire, thus gaining myself a good reputation, which in turn has safeguarded me a job for as long as I am physically capable of doing it.

My time ending at Newark Cemetery may have been a setback, but I was more than a little troubled when only a few months later, I discovered that I might also lose work at both Balderton and Farndon Cemeteries.

This was worrying, as these two cemeteries accounted for a third of the work I did each year.

This rumour was then confirmed when two ex-colleagues from Newark unexpectedly turned up one afternoon when I was working at Balderton. Oddly, they both questioned me regarding the workings of the two cemeteries.

It quickly became apparent that the two parish councils of Balderton and Farndon had been approached with a proposal for all new burials to be dug by machine, under the guidance of Newark Town Council.

Thankfully, nothing more came of this.

Then, in October 2022, I was made aware that the gravedigging at Newark Cemetery would be going out to tender again. Surprisingly, I was asked in a roundabout way if I might be interested.

Even though many of my friends and colleagues advised me to stay clear and not to get involved, it sparked my interest, and so I audaciously submitted a quotation.

Admittedly, I wasn't considering my age, or past grievances with the council. I just thought about how good it would be to go back to where it had all started.

Even more bizarrely, at the exact same time, I was also approached by Gainsborough Town Council and a funeral director from Ruskington, Lincolnshire, who were both keen on utilising my services.

But after careful consideration, I said no to both of these, and after seven months waiting for a reply regarding a possible return to Newark Cemetery, I concluded that too much time had passed and I was no longer interested. Besides, I had plenty to be getting on with.

CHAPTER 7

You've Dug It Wrong

The unfamiliar village of Hawksworth is situated approximately ten miles from Newark-on-Trent and has a population of less than 150. Only once have I dug in the churchyard there, and it's not one I'll forget easily.

In November 2010 I was asked to reopen an existing grave. The headstone – or footstone in this case – had been removed, and so I proceeded to prepare the grave. The dig was straightforward enough and not too dissimilar to other nearby villages. Rich dark topsoil changing the deeper I dug to red/bronze-coloured clay. It was heavy-going, but happily it took my colleague and me just a morning to complete.

Because I had another grave to dig at Caythorpe Cemetery, I assigned the backfilling of this to my brother Paul and my employee Gary Jones.

They waited in the van, looking on as the vicar led the funeral procession out of church to the grave. As the coffin was about to be lowered, the vicar abruptly stopped the interment, insisting that the coffin be turned around, thus placing the head at the foot end of the dig. As a result, the coffin would not fit the grave. My colleagues were hurriedly called over, and in front of everyone they endured the horrendous task of having to widen it, while the family watched on.

For my workmates, this was completely embarrassing.

Thankfully, the family took it well; in fact, they were wholly amused by it, but of course this was of little comfort to my colleagues.

When I was told what had occurred, I was fuming, as I knew I had not dug the grave incorrectly. Although the headstone had been fixed as a footstone, I had dug the grave on the usual east/west alignment.

The undertaker later confirmed that I had dug the grave correctly, though at the time they too had given my colleagues the raised-eyebrow look. Graciously, they asked me to relay their apologies to my workmates and promised to make it clear to the family what had occurred.

It is a common misconception to presume that all headstones are fixed at the head end of the grave. Many are not!

The vicar offered no apology.

CHAPTER 8

Stone on the Hill

Just three-and-a-half miles from Hawksworth, you can find the village of Flawborough. The church there is now closed for burials. However, I did once have the misfortune of preparing a grave in the churchyard.

The churchwarden was quick to inform me that Flawborough was an Old Saxon word meaning 'stone on the hill'.

Both the undertaker and their previous gravedigger had warned me that this may be a difficult job and that I shouldn't leave it to the last minute. They were not wrong. It was indeed a back-breaking, time-consuming task. It took me seven hours to prepare and complete a single-depth grave.

It was not too different to digging two miles up the road in the neighbouring village of Staunton in the Vale. I've had a few nightmares there, I can tell you. Mostly, it's a mixture of clay and stone, but at various depths you'll find what I refer to as slab bottom: solid sheets of stone.

Flawborough was slightly different, as the stone level began at a much shallower depth. I wasn't unearthing small boulders that were tightly compressed together. No, this was a continuous smooth piece of stone, which had a similar structure to slate. This ecological formation extended to an unknown depth.

Encouragingly, using a pickaxe it could be split easily, and therefore I could lift it in sheets, similar to lifting paving slabs on a patio.

Sizing and shaping the grave was my main difficulty. At one point I did find myself on my hands and knees using a hammer and bolster to chisel away the chunks of stone that stuck out from the grave walls. It was a tediously slow job, a natural ready-made stone vault.

I had never had one like this before, nor have I since. Whether I was just unlucky that day, I'll never know, but at least I won't be going there again. I hope!

CHAPTER 9

Always Expect the Unexpected

Of the many graves I have dug, one of the worst scenarios I have faced occurred during the wet summer of 2007.

On 23 June, assisted by my brother Dave, I prepared a six-foot double-depth grave in the churchyard in the village of Elston, Nottinghamshire. It was a problem-free dig on a pleasant summer's day. All was good.

Come the next day, we removed excess spoil and greened up the grave in preparation for the funeral. The hearse arrived and the service began.

Then, about 20 minutes into the service, Mick North – a retired gravedigger who was working that day as a pallbearer – came running across to me.

'The grave has filled with water,' he said, 'and both sides have collapsed.'

At first I just laughed, because he often joked that something had gone wrong.

'No, I'm not joking,' he said. 'It's all caved in, honest.'

With that bombshell, I was out the van; I grabbed the ladder and a shovel before quickly making my way to the grave. There had not been any indication that there would be a problem with this, as there had been no water and the grave had stood firm throughout, but as I got graveside I was left stunned. It was a right mess. I couldn't believe what I was seeing.

'Crikey lads,' Mick announced, 'it's the last hymn. You'd better get a move on. I'll tell the undertaker what has occurred. He'll inform the vicar, and with any luck she'll sing another hymn, which should buy you some extra time.'

To be honest, it was such a disaster that I didn't quite know where to start. Hastily, my brother removed the greens while I levelled out the infill. It was all I could do in the time I had.

It was a heart-pounding moment, a close call indeed, as we were still re-dressing the grave as the vicar led the procession out of the church.

I dared not venture too far away just in case something else happened.

To think that if either one of us had been in the grave digging, it could have been fatal.

Yes, you could argue that the grave should have been shored.

Maybe. But the land here is a combination of rugged clay and marl and does not shift. Given the power and intensity with which this crashed in, I don't think shoring would have prevented it.

In the villages of Eagle and Thorpe on the Hill, the land is constantly on the move. I was once shown a stone water trough that was said to have originally been placed at one end of the churchyard but had over time ended up at the other.

One of my biggest worries when digging has always been what would happen if I was standing in the bottom of a six-foot-deep grave and it suddenly opened up, like a sinkhole, into an open void and I just disappeared.

Ooh, that's scary!

CHAPTER 10

One Grumpy Vicar

I had been expecting a phone call from a particular Lincolnshire-based undertaker asking me to prepare a grave at Cromwell churchyard, Nottinghamshire, but that call never came. At the time I thought it was a bit odd not to have been asked, as the burial was in my area. But I was busy enough, so I thought nothing more of it.

A few days later, I was indeed contacted by that undertaker. However, while I was all geared up for the job at an easy-going Cromwell, he talked me into digging a double-depth grave at gruelling Quarrington.

An indication as to how this village digs is in the name, and believe me all of my previous visits here had been, to say the least, challenging.

Despite the undertaker's promises that this dig, which buffered up close to the church, would be sandy, I took no risks and drafted in ex-Newark gravedigger Neil Alexander, who'd occasionally helped me out.

Due to other duties, I, Neil and Choco the dog did not arrive at Quarrington churchyard until 1.30 p.m. In the shade of the church, we immediately got stuck in, and true to the undertaker's word, the dig was indeed sandier than expected.

Before my arrival, the undertaker had conveyed to me that the vicar had informed him that under no circumstances must any excess spoil be dumped in the churchyard, as it all had to be removed from site. I wasn't expecting this.

Thankfully, the funeral director had kindly arranged for a skip to be delivered. However, when the driver came, he could not leave it on the road because no licence had been applied for. Therefore, I had to stop digging and hastily wheelbarrow away a guesstimated amount of spoil while the driver patiently waited.

Annoyingly, Choco, who was just an excited puppy at the time, did nothing but bark. This soon grabbed the attention of the vicar, who just happened to turn up on site in order to investigate the source of all the commotion.

It was then that Choco somehow broke free of her leash, and as she bounded up to greet the vicar, she leapt with such force that the reverend was only able to maintain her balance by grabbing hold of a headstone.

She was fuming. Angrily, the vicar yelled at me, 'No dogs are allowed in this churchyard, so I suggest you take it out.'

'Fine,' I said. 'I'll leave you my shovel. You can dig the grave, and I'll be back tomorrow. Goodbye.'

For this, I received an unholy stare, but the vicar said no more and slowly walked away, much to Neil's amusement.

Barely half an hour passed before I was in trouble again. Not only had we unearthed a sewage pipe, which looked as if it came from the church, but the soft sand had turned to compressed limestone.

I'd barely cranked up the generator and jackhammer before the vicar returned, complaining about the noise. It was apparently so loud that she could not be heard conducting the afternoon service.

'Can you please turn off that beastly machine,' she screamed, 'and stop digging until I'm finished?'

As it turned out, I had to wait for the undertaker to arrive so that we could decide what to do about the exposed sewage pipe. On inspecting the job, the undertaker concluded there was only really one option, and that was to move and reposition the dig slightly to one side.

The deeper we got, the tougher the grave became. The easy sand, which only ran to about 30 inches, was replaced by sizeable chunks of stone. By close of play (7 p.m.), we were over five feet deep. I was pleased with what we had done and was content enough that I could scrape out a few extra inches on my return.

In all my years, I had never met such a grumpy vicar as this one.

On the day of the burial, I happened to bump into her as I was preparing to leave the churchyard. I courteously tried to exchange pleasantries, but for my sins I was totally ignored.

CHAPTER 11

I Won't Get Fooled Again

There was one particular Lincolnshire funeral director, who, I may add, no longer works in the business, who I dreaded receiving a telephone call from.

He was a nice enough chap, but over time word had gotten around that he'd had a few mishaps. If and when I was available I would help him out, but I made triply sure that I checked every bit of information before taking on the job. Even his own bearers did not speak highly of him, and indeed some gravediggers refused to work for him full stop.

One evening I received a telephone call from said undertaker begging me to help him out with a burial, as the gravedigger he had booked had cancelled at the last minute.

He asked if I could prepare a grave in Folkingham churchyard, Lincolnshire. He assured me that the grave would be near to other family plots, in one particular area of the churchyard where it was sandy, and thus easy digging.

Initially I was unsure about taking on the job, as I felt he was being somewhat vague with the truth. Nevertheless, as it had been a quiet start to July and I'd never dug in the churchyard before, I agreed to do the job.

On Saturday 2 July 2011 my brother Paul and I made the long journey out to Folkingham. I had been told that the plot would be clearly marked, but on our arrival we could find nothing. As luck would have it, there was a coffee morning in the church, so the vicar was on hand to point me in the right direction.

'The plot is at the back of the church in the new extension,' he explained. 'You can bring your machine in through the back gate.'

'I don't have a machine,' I told him. 'I dig by hand. I was told it was easy-going.'

The vicar smiled. 'Who told you that? Someone's been telling you porkie pies. You're going to struggle without a machine, because it's all stone.'

My heart sank. I'd been fooled for sure.

Fortunately, experience has taught me to expect the worst and to go prepared. Even so, despite having the jackhammer, preparing the single-depth grave, in blistering sunshine, on what turned out to be one of the hottest days of the year, was draining. If that wasn't bad enough, I felt bad for my brother, as he hurt his back early in the job.

He was in agony. He was struggling to sit, stand or walk. He suffered in silence for a long six hours. How he managed to drive us home I'll never know. Sadly, this turned out to be the last time my brother Paul and I would work together.

No wonder no other gravedigger would help out this undertaker. I did fulfil two other jobs for him, at Leasingham and Heckington. Both were problematic, and as a result I did not prepare another grave for him.

CHAPTER 12

All Saints Churchyard, Eagle

A few weeks after Christmas, I was booked to prepare a grave at All Saints Church, Eagle, Lincolnshire.

As heavy snow had been forecast, I decided that rather than being caught in a raging blizzard, I would dig this grave ahead of time. This is something I rarely do here, as the churchyard is notorious for its excessively high water table. Generally, if I have the time, I'll not prepare the grave until the day of the burial, thus lessening the problem.

Many villagers have told me that the churchyard sits on a constantly moving underground spring or stream, and as a result you rarely get any more than 40 inches deep, even during the drier summer months.

The afternoon was bitterly cold. Predictably, I found water at 14 inches. The digging was awful; it was like throwing out wet concrete. The grave was filling up quicker than I could dig it out, and as darkness fell and the snow began to fall, I had achieved a depth of just 34 inches. More snow fell overnight. Although picturesque, snow only adds to a gravedigger's woes.

Back on site, once the grave was pumped out, try as I might I only managed to scrape out a few more inches, as it was filling up quicker than a running bath. The difficulties of burying in this type of land are known to locals. The families are always apprised of the situation, and on this occasion they were happy to continue.

The vicar was fully aware of the problems I was having and duly informed me that the service would be around 25 minutes long. With this in mind, I continually pumped out the grave until the very last minute, before throwing in some shavings and withdrawing to my van.

It was a further 20 minutes before they arrived at the graveside. I was restless, as I knew the water was rising fast. I had half expected to be called over to pump it out again, but oddly the burial went ahead regardless.

By the time I got to start backfilling the grave, the coffin was floating. Quickly shovelling spoil on top of the coffin held it down, but water was now overflowing the grave.

At this point the vicar arrived. He made it quite clear that he was displeased not just with the grave's depth but with the amount of water in it.

'I suggest that next time you come and dig a grave here,' he said, 'you attempt to get it a bit deeper.'

I wasn't happy with his needless comment, as he knew the score here, and so I abruptly replied, 'Yeah, I'll be sure to bring my snorkel and flippers next time. Besides, you knew how quick the water was coming in and you assured me that you would only be 25 minutes in church.'

With that, he quietly walked away.

Once I'd sufficiently covered the coffin with spoil, I hurriedly placed concrete paving slabs on top, thus sealing the grave. This was the best I could do in the circumstances. I remember thinking, as I finished up, I hope nobody stands on the grave, because if they do they'll sink to their knees.

Chapter 13

Plot 15H

After spending three arduous hours digging a grave up on the Lincolnshire Edge, the last thing I wanted to hear was 'I'm sorry, but I'm afraid you've dug it in the wrong place.'

I had arrived early in this Lincolnshire village only to find that since my last visit not only had a lock been fitted to the main entrance, but the inner cemetery gates were now also tightly secured. No one had informed me of this, and I had not been given a key.

Luckily, I did not have long to wait before the caretaker opened up. However, once on site, I discovered that despite being assured that the plot was marked, it hadn't been.

I was not in the least surprised by my findings, as it was often the case here, though it was frustrating, as I needed to crack on with the job.

I wasn't prepared to hang around for 90 minutes until the council office opened, so I opted to find it for myself. I had been given the plot number, but cross-referencing the grave spaces wasn't easy, as everything was out of line.

Due to bedrock, they only dug single side-by-side graves in this cemetery, which meant everything was a bit skew-whiff.

After careful consideration and referencing of other plot numbers, I confidently chose what I believed to be grave-space 15H, and with that I promptly got stuck in.

The gruelling stone dig was close to completion when a representative from the council turned up in order to mark the grave. After finding her bearings, she concluded that the grave I was digging was actually plot 14H and was in fact a reserved space, and therefore the wrong one.

I was not best pleased, as time was of the essence, but as I'd jumped the gun, I had no choice but to backfill it and start a fresh dig.

On this occasion my impatience had gotten the better of me. The lady from the council said, 'We don't mark the plots too early here, because children have been known to swap the markers and in the past it has caused mistakes.'

The interment was a first for me. It was a Chinese Buddhist burial, which often meant the grave was dug the opposite way around. Prior to digging, I had discussed this with the funeral director, who could not clarify it either way. As the family had not requested it,

I was told to dig the grave on the normal east/west alignment.

Fingers crossed that the undertaker was right, as it would be a difficult task to correct on the day.

When the hearse and cortège arrived, I watched in astonishment as a lady got out of her car and immediately collapsed, falling backwards onto the grass. There was uproar among the mourners as they all rushed to assist her.

Some 25 minutes later, the funeral director came across to me.

'I'm sorry,' he said, 'they'll be a while yet. It seems the spirit of the deceased has entered the daughter, and through her, she wishes to say her individual goodbyes.'

There was not much I could say to that.

In the intervening time, I spoke with the bearers. They told me how the family had given each of them a lucky bag. In it was a boiled sweet, a piece of fern and a 10-pence coin.

As the coffin was being lowered into the ground, the family turned away, so as not to watch the interment. Incense sticks were lit and pre-prepared food was placed near to the grave.

Before the funeral director departed, he said, 'The family have left a set of chopsticks by the grave. They would appreciate it if you could use them to backfill with.'

I smiled at him and said, 'Yes, of course I will.'

I once dug a grave here on the eve of the Waddington airshow. Wag the dog was with me that day. The cemetery backs on to the airfield and is directly in line with the flight path. From the moment we arrived, Wag and I were deafened by practising jets, helicopters, etc. It was intense.

Poor old Wag was a nervous wreck, cowering on the floor. It was all too much for his sensitive ears. As I couldn't put him through that, I promptly packed up and went home.

It was loud!

CHAPTER 14

Is Everything Alright?

I'd only dug at St Mary's churchyard in Orston twice before, but both times had been problematic. The land is not easy to work, especially during the dry summer months, as it's clay. From the very moment I was booked for this job I knew it would be a long, exhausting challenge, and I was not wrong.

I had been told that the plot I was to dig had been marked and was located at the back of the church. On my initial walk around, however, I couldn't pinpoint anything at all. Only by sheer chance did I stumble upon a broken tree branch that had been loosely shoved into the ground. It was primitive marking, but it was obvious that it had been intentionally placed.

As I checked the area, my original fears of it being a tricky dig were confirmed.

At one end of the plot stood a centuries-old horse chestnut tree, and at the other sprawled an overgrown ewe tree. Glancing at the area beneath the two, it was obvious that the earth had received very little in the way of moisture or sunlight for many years. The ground was parched, cracked and overgrown with ivy.

Like most churchyards, there were no vacant unused plots here. The likelihood that this plot had been used previously was extremely high. In actual fact, I was banking on this, as it would make my life somewhat easier.

Unluckily for me, the family had requested a double-depth grave (six feet).

Although the top was crumbly and relatively loose, progress was slow.

Not only was I foiled by tree root after tree root, some as thick as my thigh, but during the course of the dig I inadvertently disturbed several nests of red ants, which led to them swarming everywhere.

The dig was alive. They were all over me – in my boots, socks and clothing. They weren't half annoying and extremely painful.

The majority of my time, however, was spent chopping my way through a mass of thickly knotted roots that were tightly interwoven, criss-crossing for pretty much the whole depth of the dig. The rest of my time was spent jackhammering out chunks of limestone in order to reach an acceptable depth.

In all, it took me two five-hour sessions to complete.

On the day of the interment, I greened up the grave before going to wait in the van. Before the hearse arrived, the vicar and two bearers came to see where the grave was. I was parked close by and in earshot of both the parties and so could easily hear what they were discussing.

It was then that I overheard the vicar say, 'I don't think that's big enough, never mind deep enough. What do you think?'

I knew the bearers quite well, and so I was surprised when I heard one of them say, 'I've seen deeper, and, yes, it does look extremely small.'

I thought, you cheeky buggers, there's nothing wrong with that.

I would have assumed that if anyone had any doubts, they would have at least come and spoken to me. It's far better to deal with any problems before the interment than during.

Concerned by what they had said, I jumped out of my van and asked, 'Is everything alright?'

Both parties looked directly at me and nodded, and the vicar replied, 'Everything appears to be fine, thank you.'

Even after 40-plus years in the trade, when I hear that my work is being questioned, I can't help but go into worry mode. My paperwork specified a coffin that was six foot three by 22 inches with uplift bar handles. My grave measured six foot ten by 29 inches, and there was ample depth for a double grave.

I didn't need to convince myself, but the seed of doubt had been planted and I was on edge.

I spent a nervy 45 minutes waiting for the church service to finish. As they arrived at the graveside, I sat and watched while the undertaker pulled away the putlogs and bearers began to lower the coffin.

At this point, I took a deep breath and closed my eyes. There was a pause, a moment's silence, before the vicar began to recite prayers. I opened my eyes to see the bearers retreating to the sidelines. What a relief! After an anxious wait, the coffin was safely interred.

When I removed the green sheets, I could see there was ample clearance around the coffin. For my own peace of mind, I measured from the top of the coffin to the top of the grave, and it was exactly four feet four inches. Ample depth for a future reopen dig.

CHAPTER 15

Stuck in the Mud

All Saints Church in Coddington, Nottinghamshire, has always made my top-10 list of tough-digging, avoid-if-you-can graveyards. It's not a place I like to dig, especially unaccompanied. I would go as far as to say that it has some of the worst ground I have had the displeasure of working in.

The last row of virgin ground, which borders the bottom boundary wall, has taken 10 years to fill and has been formidable digging the whole time. I once started a six-foot double here at 1 p.m., finished at 10 p.m., and returned at 6 a.m. in order to complete the job in time.

For the most part, the churchyard is made up of heavy solid clay mixed with sporadic layers of limestone, and depending on your location there is a fair chance you'll hit water.

Working in torrential rain, I once prepared a grave that was just a sodden heap of sticky slop. Backfilling the next day, I found myself on my hands and knees, hand-balling the wet clay back into the grave, as it was so waterlogged it could not be shovelled.

Nowadays, the last remaining area being used is where the old orchard was. This is in the vicinity of a natural underground spring. Over time, this has been backfilled with all sorts of rubbish. From graveyard litter to farmyard debris, you can unearth just about anything, including animal bones.

I had allowed myself two digging days to complete this job, but astonishingly it took me just six hours. The top three feet was soft, made-up ground, so I was spared the laborious task of having to chisel it out with a jackhammer.

A wetter-than-average winter had paid dividends. The allocated plot was slightly higher up a slope, and for the most part it wasn't a bad dig, though at five feet six inches I located the spring.

On the day of the burial, I climbed down into the grave to bail it out. As my feet hit the bottom, I was immediately sucked down into thick sludge which quickly engulfed my wellies. No matter how much I tried, I could not free my legs and feet. I was beginning to panic, though I was able to reach the ladder and so could climb out, minus my footwear.

After putting on my work boots, I found myself precariously dangling off the ladder as I tried to retrieve my wellingtons. For a time, I didn't think I'd be able to free them, because the thick mud was slowly pulling them down. Eventually, I managed to recover them. I then had the same problem with the ladder. Standing on it had pushed it further down and it had become trapped. To free it, I simultaneously rocked it back and forth, and ultimately it dislodged itself.

Water or no water, there was no way I was going back into the grave, so I obscured the bottom with generous shavings, placed the green matting down, and waited for the funeral party to arrive.

In all my years, I have never come across sinking mud like this. I wonder if the coffin got swallowed up.

CHAPTER 16

My Close Encounter with Death

Monday 17 October 2011 is a day that I'd rather forget, as it's the day that I came within a hair's breadth of killing myself.

I was preparing a grave at All Saints Church in my home village of Swinderby, Lincolnshire, when, without warning, I unearthed what appeared to be an old water pipe.

My first thought was that this pipework must have crossed three other rows of graves. With that in mind, I assumed that other gravediggers must also have stumbled upon it, and as it was loosely laid in the ground, I deduced that it must have been disconnected and long forgotten about.

Strangely, something told me to leave it well alone and just to realign the grave's position. This was what I planned to do. But as the pipework crossed much of the dig, it was impossible, as it was in the way. Ignoring my inner feelings, I continued to excavate around it.

Hindsight, of course, is a great thing, but in real time I made the wrong choice.

As I hacked away spoil from the end of the grave, I unintentionally struck the exposed pipework, and within a flash it exploded. There was a gush of white light, and I was propelled back to the foot end of the grave. This was followed by a second explosion. Thankfully, I'd jumped clear by then.

I was immediately thrown into disarray, as I didn't know what to do first. Earlier on I had noticed that both the vicar and the churchwarden were in the graveyard, standing by the church. All I could think of was to cover the grave over and go and find some help.

There was a coffee morning in the church, and as I arrived villagers were anxiously discussing why all the power had gone off.

I explained that that was probably down to me, as I had accidentally spliced into an electric cable while digging a grave in the churchyard.

They all stood there in total silence, looking bemused. Not one of them asked if I was OK.

After contacting the power company's emergency hotline, two vans and six men promptly arrived. They completed an initial inspection of the site. None of the workmen could believe that not only had I survived to tell the tale, but I hadn't received any serious burns either.

One of the workmen was so gobsmacked that he actually handed me a pound coin and said, 'You do know that you should be dead. If you have that much luck, then you'd better go and put this pound on tonight's lottery.'

It turned out that the power cable carried around 11,500 volts and had been laid in the 1930s. Unfortunately, none of the churchyard plans showed it. To some extent, it was still the main power supply to the village. In my moment of madness, not only had I blacked out half the community, but I'd stopped the trains on the line between Nottingham and Lincoln.

Over the years, I have unearthed numerous services, including gas pipes, floodlight cables, sewage pipes, mains water pipes ... The list is endless. However, I'm usually very careful. On this occasion, I was fooled by something that really did not appear to be what it actually was.

I had been stupid, and it could have been fatal. Very often, graves here fill with water. If that had been the case, I most certainly would not be here now.

As the power company began repairing the cable, I was left with the task of digging a second grave.

While doing this, I saw a white rabbit hop past at the end of the dig. Was I really still in the land of the living? I had to actually pinch myself, just to be sure that I was still alive.

Happily, it turned out that the rabbit had escaped from the nearby school. I wouldn't have known, except a member of staff shouted over the fence, 'Have you seen a white rabbit? One of the children has left the hutch open.'

What a relief!

Many years earlier, in the same churchyard, a gravedigger found a metal object that he set to one side. Unsure of what he'd found, he duly removed it from site, only to discover that it was a small unexploded bomb. That's the last thing you'd want bouncing about in the back of your van.

CHAPTER 17

Grafting in a Downpour

After completing a late afternoon backfill in the village of East Stoke, Nottinghamshire, I made my way across for an evening dig out at Leadenham, Lincolnshire.

Only on that very morning had I been asked by a Nottingham-based funeral director if I could assist them, as their gravedigger had been taken ill.

All afternoon, storm clouds had been gathering, and by the time I reached my destination there was thunder and lightning and it was pouring with rain. I waited in the van, hoping that the summer storm would pass, but there was to be no let-up. It was in for the evening.

I had no choice but to pull on my coat and face the worst of Mother Nature.

Leadenham churchyard is not a place you can dig quickly. It's tough-going. Due to the severity of the weather, I did not dare crank up the generator and jackhammer, so for near on three hours I toiled, gouging out the stone with my pick and shovel.

Driving home in soggy wet joggers with my sweatshirt and T-shirt stuck to my body was unpleasant. It's not like I hadn't been caught in the rain before, but this was excessive.

My morale was low. On returning to my home village, I fortuitously saw the weekly mobile fish and chip shop. What a sight for an empty belly.

Wow, did that pie, chips and gravy go down a treat. It certainly brought a smile back to my face.

It's always a good feeling when you return to a job to discover that you've actually got it deeper than you thought you had. All that was left for me to do was bottom it out, straighten the sides and check my measurements.

After the mourners had filed into church, the undertaker appeared and promptly headed in my direction.

'Hi there,' he said, as I wound down my window. 'I'm a bearer down today. Will you please help me out? Will you either be on hand to lower the coffin, or, if I assist the lads, will you pull out the putlogs?'

I didn't relish doing either, but I agreed to do the latter. Putlogs are the wooden struts that cross the grave, on which the coffin rests before being lowered into the ground.

From time to time I do get asked to do this. It's not something I like to do, as the sudden appearance of a grubby-looking gravedigger in his muddy boots, standing graveside, can be a bit unsightly.

I've had some terrible digs at St Swithun's Church, Leadenham.

In 2013 I was asked to prepare a reopen burial. I was on top of the first coffin that had been interred at just 28 inches deep. I contacted the undertaker and was told that come what may, the family were adamant that the plot be used. After the second burial, the lid of the coffin was just 13 inches from the surface. I had to wrap the coffin in polythene and place concrete paving slabs on top to seal it.

To this day, I believe that like most burials here, the grave was originally dug as a single depth. I think someone messed up, especially as there was a reserved space next to it.

CHAPTER 18

Beware the Rare Tall Thrift Plant

In July 2016 I received a telephone call asking me if I would prepare a double-depth grave at Ancaster Cemetery, Lincolnshire.

Initially, I cringed at the thought, because in the past I had dug around that area, and I knew the village was surrounded by numerous stone quarries.

Sensing my hesitation, the undertaker proceeded to explain that machine digging was prohibited in the cemetery; therefore, all graves had to be hand-dug. He assured me that digging was light, workable and trouble-free.

Hmm, I had been fed this spiel many times before. Yet on this occasion I had total faith in what I was being told.

It turned out that machines were not allowed in the cemetery because Ancaster is rich in Roman archaeology. Additionally, Natural England had declared the cemetery to be a designated site of special interest due to the existence of the rare Tall Thrift plant, which grows nowhere else in the UK apart from Ancaster Cemetery. Unfortunately, it is now in decline there too.

I was quite intrigued by the cemetery's history, and having not visited before, I couldn't wait to see what all the fuss was about.

On Saturday 14 July I met with the cemetery groundsman. He was certainly informative. He was passionate and extremely specific about where I should stand, walk, run my barrow and place my groundsheet and walk-boards. He constantly scrutinised my every move, making sure I didn't flatten or crush any plants.

I was more than happy to be guided by him, and I fully adhered to his requests. However, he was an extremely difficult man to please. All was fine until he began telling me how to do my job.

At one point, it got a bit fraught between us, when he tried to tell me that the double-depth grave had to be a minimum of eight feet deep.

'No,' I told him, 'six feet is the norm and that is more than adequate.'

He made it quite clear that he was not happy about this, and he stormed off vowing to check burial law. On his return, he simply said, 'I will allow it this time.'

As promised, it turned out to be a relatively straightforward dig. I found no Roman burials, cremation urns or other archaeological artefacts, and I did not disturb the all-important Tall Thrift plant.

As I finished up and climbed out of the grave, the groundsman appeared.

'Have you finished?' he said. 'If so, then I need to check the depth before you leave.'

He pulled out his tape measure.

'Yes. Six foot six. Yes, I'm happy with that. Thank you.'

Only a few weeks later, I returned in order to prepare another grave. I wasn't looking forward to confronting the all-knowing groundsman. However, on this occasion, although he was visibly loitering about, keeping an eye on me, he left me to get on with my work.

Ancaster Cemetery was indeed an interesting place. I hoped I'd get asked back again, but as yet I never have been.

CHAPTER 19

The Old Rectory Courtyard

Elston churchyard in Nottinghamshire is one of those places where you dare not leave the digging until the very last minute, as it can easily catch you out. Generally speaking, it's awkward but fairly good-going. However, as gravedigger Mick North always used to say, 'The land is changeable here. Always go prepared and take your jackhammer, 'cause you never know.'

When I saw the chosen spot for this double-depth dig, I was relieved, because it was adjacent to two other digs I had done not long before, and both had been reasonably good digging.

That said, I noticed that the plot selected was close to where the old rectory had once stood. Mick had already informed me that a wall which had originally bordered the rectory had once stood close to where I was digging, and looking at the compacted rubble I was removing, I guessed I was on top of it.

Mick had often told of the problems he had encountered here, and, like him, time and again, I had painstakingly toiled to remove the old cobbled courtyard which remained preserved and intact some 20 inches or so under the turf.

Rain and shine I battled with this grave for 16 hours in order to reach the required depth, and it never once got any easier. The deep layer of limestone, bricks, holly roots and other bits of debris ran to a depth of four feet. The remaining two feet was a solid dry layer of marl. Neither my pickaxe nor the jackhammer had any real impact. Digging it was simply down to brute force, patience and perseverance.

On my second day of digging this, it was reported that 33 mm of rain had fallen throughout Nottinghamshire. I can vouch for that, as I got soaked.

By 2022, the last of the remaining vacant spaces had pretty much been filled. Still, as the church has yet to decide where it will go next, I'm sure it will try to squeeze in a few more customers.

CHAPTER 20

When Death Comes to Call

For most people, digging out a grave for a close family member would be a daunting task and not something they would ever envisage themselves doing. But when my father died, I had no anxieties about preparing his grave. It was the last thing I could ever do for him.

Admittedly, gravedigging is my profession, and so to some extent I was able to emotionally detach myself from the grief that it brings. Nevertheless, when death comes to call, you can't help but view it from a completely different perspective, one you are never fully prepared for.

My family has always spoken openly about death, and, oddly, in the weeks prior to my father's passing, he had actually asked me if, when the time came, I would dig his grave. It was Christmas. I kind of laughed it off. But in the back of my mind, I knew he wasn't a well man, although I don't think any of us really knew how poorly he actually was.

When I found out that my dad had passed away, I had just arrived at Swinderby churchyard. Words can't express how I felt at that time. Everything seemingly went into slow motion. Needless to say, I was saddened by his passing, but after taking a personal moment, I got on with digging another grave. It was all very surreal.

At 10.30 a.m. on 10 February 2015, I met with my brother Dave, who had travelled across from Wessington, Derbyshire, in order to assist me with the digging. We discussed many topics. One thing we both agreed was a bit weird was that our dad had been in King's Mill Hospital, on level 4, ward 44. Bizarrely, this was my 4,044th grave.

I had been unable to sleep most of the night, fretting about the cemetery's high water table. I had dug there only two weeks prior, and the water table had certainly hampered proceedings. As my father's grave was situated just two plots away, I presumed it would be equally as wet.

Astonishingly, we were able to reach a depth which was usually achievable only during the drier summer months. I joked with my brother that Dad must have had a word with Moses, thus parting the tide. I was relieved.

I would like to thank long-term friend and ex-work colleague Gary Jones who put forward his services to backfill the grave.

Thank you. It was much appreciated.

Every now and then, I receive a request from a family member, asking if they could come and partly assist me with the digging of their loved one's grave. Only a few have ever assisted. Many have a last-minute change of heart and do not arrive, and there are those who help out for half an hour before withdrawing from site.

Over the years, my services have been personally requested through various funeral directors, and this is always a source of pride. People seemingly get comfort not just from knowing the gravedigger, but from being secure in the knowledge that they can rely on me to complete the job with both professionalism and dignity.

This I'm proud of.

CHAPTER 21

One of Those Days

Spring 2012 had been wetter than usual. The water table was high and the land was saturated. From April to July, I endured many problems. The ground was unable to support itself, and despite many digs being shored, grave after grave toppled in.

The day began with a rare trip out to the Church of Our Lady of Egmanton, Nottinghamshire. I'd been asked to prepare a double grave in the cemetery opposite the church. At the best of times, the land here can be difficult to dig. It mostly consists of a well-compacted mixture of lumpy red clay and jagged stone. The land is not too dissimilar to the neighbouring villages of Laxton and Tuxford. All three are tediously slow to dig and will challenge your ability to complete your task. These three churchyards will guarantee you a sleepless night.

Working alone, I had two burials that day. In the morning I dressed the grave at Egmanton before whizzing across to Caunton village, where I made ready for the day's first interment.

I'd just begun to backfill this grave when I received a telephone call from an extremely worried undertaker who proceeded to tell me that the grave at Egmanton had collapsed and asked if I could go over and sort it as the family were already in church.

Adhering to procedure meant that I couldn't just leave Caunton uncovered. I hastily buried the coffin with soil and covered it over with walk-boards, thus obscuring it from view.

Once I'd accomplished this, I sped across to Egmanton. In the midst of a heavy thunderous downpour, I arrived with minutes to spare.

What I found was a big gaping hole on one side, as a result of which the grave had half-filled itself.

In the pouring rain I threw back the green sheets and commenced clearing it out. The immediate area was too unstable to achieve the full dig, but in the time allowed I was able to re-dig it to the safest depth possible. I had everything crossed that it wouldn't cave in again, and luckily it did behave itself.

It was a couple of hours before I got to return to Caunton churchyard. Back on site, I quickly continued where I'd left off. I had only just got stuck in when the family returned to view the flowers. As they reached the graveside, they made it quite clear to me that they were not happy that the job was not yet complete.

All I could do was apologise for the delay. If only they'd known the day I'd had.

CHAPTER 22

An Open-Cast Mine

It was a beautiful warm sunny April morning and my brother Paul, Wag the dog and I were journeying to the village of Tibshelf in Derbyshire.

I was concerned about the challenge ahead. It was way out of my normal area and miles from home. I was worried about completing a double-depth dig in just the one visit, but I really needed to, as the village was too far to travel to numerous times.

As no one had been forthcoming regarding what the digging was like, we packed the van full with everything we might require, thus allowing for all eventualities. From extra shore boards and shoring equipment to jackhammer and generator, we took the lot.

At the council office in Tibshelf I was met by a somewhat cranky official who handed me a plan of the cemetery, which marked the plot we were to dig, and then swiftly shepherded me out of the building.

I think I was seen as the out-of-town gravedigger who was poaching someone else's work, which was unfair.

I would have preferred for the local gravedigger to have done this, because they would have had an eye for the land and would have known what to expect. I didn't know why the funeral director had asked me to do it in the first place.

The cemetery, set on the outskirts of the village, was relatively new. Fortunately, the grave we were to dig was on level ground near to the main road and car park. Beyond this, the land sloped steeply downhill, and at the bottom there was a stream. I thought this was strange, as the cemetery appeared not to have been suitably landscaped, but little did I know ...

Despite the dig progressing well, it was proving to be a more arduous task than expected. By early afternoon, we were both waning somewhat. Being miles from home meant the pressure was on to get it finished, as neither of us could afford to allocate a second day's digging. The compacted mixture of grey clay and stone was moveable with a jackhammer, though it was irritatingly slow-going.

Then, quite out of the blue, a van towing a mini digger arrived on site, speedily pulling up near to where we were working. Out jumped a man and his female companion, and immediately we were drawn into conversation. He announced that he was the local gravedigger and was unaware of our visit.

Whoops!

'I'm utterly gobsmacked,' he said, on viewing our handiwork. 'I can't believe that you've been sent all the way here to dig by hand. This used to be an open-cast mine and it's been backfilled with all kinds of rubbish. We've found huge blocks of concrete and thick steel cables, and even my machine struggles at times.'

With that, he praised our progress, before jumping on his digger and proceeding to dig out another grave, which I may add he completed in double-quick time.

Before leaving, he came over to us.

'Please don't be offended,' he said, 'but whilst I'm here, would you like me to scoop out the rest of your dig, leaving you to shape up and finish off?'

Now, normally, I would not even consider the idea. But on this occasion, time and distance were against us, so amiably I accepted his kind offer.

As his bucket reached deeper into the earth, he hauled out some chunky pieces of stone which Paul and I would undoubtedly have battled with well into the evening.

This fellow gravedigger's timely intervention had saved the day. It meant that for once, Paul and I got home at a reasonable hour. Even Wag was pleased.

Hopefully, I never get asked to go back there. I do not recall his name, but whoever that gravedigger was, thank you.

CHAPTER 23

Never Be Complacent

I've dug more than my fair share of graves at St Helen's Church, Brant Broughton, Lincolnshire. It is known for being a relatively straightforward dig, as this God's acre has been dug and re-dug numerous times. Like in many churchyards, the water table governs the depth. Most burials here are now on the south side of the church, where the headstones have been removed and the land reclaimed. The majority are singles that take no more than a couple of hours to complete.

On this day, the plot I was to prepare was on the north side, beside a dominant tree which, when in leaf, would have overshadowed the entire area. From just looking at the grave's position and its proximity to the tree, it was obvious that I had gone unprepared.

At a depth of two feet, I not only struck tree roots but hit upon a hard crust of limestone. Bearing in mind that I was a good few miles away from the infamous Lincolnshire Edge, I was surprised.

Manually, with just my pickaxe, I could not for the life of me break through the stone crust, and so, somewhat despondent, I journeyed back to Collingham to fetch the necessary tools.

Annoyingly, back on site, neither of my two demolition hammers would strike up. This may have been down to them being stored in a damp lock-up. For the next 90 minutes I persevered, though I achieved very little. The ground just would not budge. I was ready to call it a day when I thought, I'll give the jackhammer one more try. Unbelievably, after an afternoon airing in the sunshine, it fired up at the first attempt. With renewed vigour I got stuck in, and like a knife through butter I was able to smash my way through the stone layer. However, once I'd removed the stone, the dig turned into a quagmire of mud and rising water.

Spookily, from that day to this, that jackhammer has never worked again. I think someone was looking out for me that afternoon.

Note to self: just because the graveyard you're visiting is usually an easy dig, don't assume that your next job will be – so go prepared!

The grave was for a celebrity sportsman, a British international showjumper who had represented his country no fewer than 25 times. I felt quite honoured to have been associated with a distinguished celebrity's burial. Although I did not recognise anyone at the committal, I was told there were a number of famous people in attendance.

Chapter 24

Eight Days a Week

One of the downsides of being a gravedigger is that I rarely get to have a holiday, especially for any length of time, as cover is not always available. Even when I do manage to take time out, I can guarantee that at some point during my break, I will be contacted.

Imagine my surprise when on 27 December 2010, while relaxing in my hotel room high up in the Black Forest mountains in Germany, my phone rang and a Lincolnshire undertaker asked, 'Can I book you to dig a grave, please?'

To my further surprise, I was contacted by another funeral director as I waited to board the ferry home.

My wife was not amused.

As it turned out, these were just two of the 21 bookings plus a further pair of interments of ashes that I was asked to prepare in the first month of 2011.

Sunday 2 January

No sooner had I arrived home from Germany than I was out preparing a double-depth grave at Balderton

Cemetery. Digs at Flintham, Caunton, Norwell, Newark and Beckingham quickly followed over the next few days.

Thursday 6 January

After completing backfills at Flintham and Newark Cemetery, I hot-footed it across to Beckingham, though I did not arrive until late afternoon, by which time darkness was descending.

I was somewhat relieved that this was a reopen dig, although this was unusual, as the churchyard was renowned for its high water table. It could have been worse; it could have been situated near to where the old stable block once stood. There, I would have had to dig through foundations and cobbled floors, which was no easy task.

Under floodlights I grafted in the freezing cold rain into the early evening. Progress was extremely slow. I was tired, and every shovel became an effort to lift. It had been a long, back-breaking day, and by 7 p.m. I was cold to the core. As I physically could do no more, I called it a day.

Working alone in the blackness of a churchyard doesn't particularly bother me, but you do become aware that you can only see within the distance of the floodlights. This can be discomforting, as you feel that you're being watched.

It's easy to become disorientated with your surroundings, and when you switch off those lights, you're at the mercy of the churchyard.

It's best to plan your exit route in advance, because there are so many hidden obstacles that if you stray from your track, you could quite easily end up at A & E.

Friday 7 January

Three backfills at Norwell, Beckingham and Caunton, after which I raced across to Farndon to prepare another grave, again in fading daylight.

Saturday 8 January

After completing a Saturday backfill at Farndon, I rushed back to Newark Cemetery to help Gary Jones with the digging of a double-depth grave. This was for a 33-stone man.

Sunday 9 January

With no rest for the wicked, my brother Paul, Gary Jones and I travelled to Cotgrave, Nottinghamshire, where we quickly prepared a single-depth burial. Later that afternoon, I went off alone and prepared another grave at Balderton Cemetery.

It had been a tiring, full-on week – and the week ahead was not much easier, with another seven burials, including another hefty man, this time weighing 23 stone.

Nowadays, when I scroll back through my diaries, I do often wonder how we did it all.

CHAPTER 25

Hill Top Cemetery, Gonerby

It wasn't often that the wife assisted me with my work, but when she was available her support was greatly appreciated. She didn't do digging but would happily drive, cast back spoil, dress, backfill, and lay out wreaths, all of which saved time.

Although I'd dug in Gonerby churchyard, this was my first time at the newly opened cemetery, which was situated high up on a hill. The views overlooking Newark and pretty much the whole of the Trent Valley were superb. The day was cold, sunny and clear and you could see for miles.

A plaque in the cemetery revealed that during the Second World War, an observation post was sited here which also included an ammunition depot. I could see why, as it would have been an ideal position for spotting enemy aircraft.

My wife laughed.

'Oh no, not a munitions depot,' she said. 'If anyone's going to unearth anything left behind, then, with your track record, it's going to be you.'

'Yes,' I joshed, 'how deep did you want the grave, Mr Undertaker? Is 20 feet deep by 20 feet wide big enough?'

The downside of being on an exposed hill was that you were open to the elements. It was bright, breezy and freezing cold, with intermittent sleet and snow showers, which were a frequent hindrance and not welcome.

My wife is a hardy soul and was well accustomed to working outside, but after a couple of hours, frozen to the core, she gave in and went and sat in the warm van, vowing never to help me again.

This was to be a double-depth grave, and although it came out fairly easy, at 43 inches it suddenly filled with water. I immediately reported my finding to the undertaker. He was somewhat surprised by this and promptly went off to speak to both the family and the cemetery supervisor.

The family were sympathetic and were more than happy to reserve the adjacent plot for future use. The cemetery supervisor, however, was stunned by my findings.

On her arrival, she stood there staring into the open grave. 'Groundwater, on a hill? We had extensive test holes dug to a depth of six feet, and no water was found. It doesn't make sense.'

It turned out that the test holes had been dug at the height of summer, at a time when the whole country was experiencing a prolonged drought and rivers and reservoirs were at an all-time low. Following this, the autumn and winter had been exceedingly wet, and as clay traps and holds water, I for one was not at all surprised by the situation, especially as in the days leading up to this, I had prepared jobs at Syerston, Claypole and Brant Broughton, and they too had filled with water.

As I could do no more, the grave was closed down. When I returned to Gonerby the next morning, I was astonished to discover that the water in the grave had frozen. This was a first!

The water level itself had not risen any higher, but I had not expected it to be covered in a thin layer of ice.

How I wish I had taken the pump with me, because it was blooming freezing stood in the grave in my leaky wellingtons, hand-bailing out 60 gallons of ice-cold water. Ooh, my feet were cold!

CHAPTER 26

You Got Deeper than
the Last Gravedigger

The day before I was due to prepare this particular grave, I had laboured with a single-depth grave at Stow Cemetery, Lincolnshire. Less than 24 hours later, I was to find myself just down the road, in the village of Saxilby.

This was the last of four graves – including one in Marton and another at Saxilby – which I had only agreed to do in order to help out the undertaker, on the understanding this was a one-off favour while they found a suitable replacement for their regular gravedigger, who had quit without any warning.

I'd dug in the churchyard here a number of times and knew that it was likely to be a difficult dig, especially as it had to be double depth.

Saxilby churchyard is either exceptionally wet, thus filling with water at two feet, or extremely dry and unbreakable due to the red-clay land baking so hard. Although it was mid-November, it was the latter I was facing.

Assisting me on this daunting challenge was a young lad called Ben. He had been helping me for a few weeks, but nothing could have prepared him for this.

What little moisture there was, was captured within the turf. Underneath, it was bone dry. Only the jackhammer had any real impact, though even the powered help struggled to break it up.

Slowly, slowly, we dug the grave, but by the end of day one we were barely four feet deep. Ben was on his knees. It had certainly gotten the better of him. He was uncharacteristically quiet, and I fully expected him to decline an additional day's work. Happily, though, he agreed to give it another go, and so we arranged to meet at first light.

Although we had five hours to finish the dig, the stubborn dry clay was proving difficult to remove. It became a race against time to complete the dig to a reasonable depth. In fact, I was still shaping and levelling the grave as the funeral cortège arrived and the family went into church.

While I was greening up, the village groundsman showed up. He pulled up alongside me, stopped his ride-on mower, got off and peered down into the grave. He looked at me and said, 'Wow, I'm amazed. You've done well. You're deeper than the last gravedigger got, and he had a machine.'

I welcomed the man's praise, as it had certainly been a horrible, back-breaking job. Definitely the worst job that I'd completed there. And, yes, there was a moment when I really thought it was going to beat me.

Further adding to my woes, I discovered that the funeral director had added six inches' clearance to the coffin size given to me. Not knowing this, I had added my usual seven-inch safety size, which meant there was over a foot clearance all around.

I was annoyed to say the least, for in tough ground like this, the last thing you need is unwarranted digging. This wasn't the first time that this undertaker had overcompensated on the size, but it sure was their last. I never accepted any further work from them.

CHAPTER 27

Whoops, I Pegged Out
the Wrong Grave

On my previous visit to Normanton on Trent Cemetery, Nottinghamshire, the adjacent field had been flooded near on up to its perimeter hedge. This was not uncommon, as the cold wet winter months often left the heavy clay land waterlogged, spongy and difficult to work.

In this cemetery, the ground had been raised up with a couple of feet of imported spoil, without which you'd have been hard-pressed to get any real depth at all.

Four months on from my last visit, I arrived at the cemetery just as the sun was emerging and the previous night's frost was beginning to evaporate. It was a beautiful still morning, perfect for digging. The land was exactly the right consistency. No need for the jackhammer or pickaxe; the damp clay carved out easily with a shovel. With no rising groundwater in sight, I managed to achieve a respectable depth, with the added bonus of it taking me little more than three hours to complete. Win, win. I was well pleased.

Unluckily, my joy was rather short-lived.

Early the following morning, I received a telephone call from Normanton's parish clerk, informing me that there had been a mix-up, an admin error, resulting in the wrong grave being marked.

The parish clerk sheepishly said, 'I have now correctly repegged it. I'll leave it with you. It's now in your hands.'

And with no apology whatsoever, the lady proceeded to hang up.

Disappointingly, this meant that through no fault of mine, I would have to return to Normanton in order to backfill and reinstate the grave before digging out another.

At the time of the call, I was greening up a grave at East Stoke in readiness for a burial. By the time I'd completed my backfill and sped across to Normanton, dusk was setting in. I had just enough time to backfill and reinstate the grave and start the new dig before all light was lost.

I returned early the following morning and wasted no time in throwing out the remainder of the dig. I finished with just an hour to spare.

Bizarrely, I had a similar incident just a few weeks later at Beckingham churchyard.

CHAPTER 28

Graveside Catastrophe

The days leading up to me preparing this grave had been hot, dry and oppressive. Then, on the evening prior to the burial, the weather changed and summer storms began moving in. In the early hours, I lay in bed listening to heavy rain as it bounced off the windows, and I thought, Ian, you're in trouble.

I had prepared a double-depth grave at North Clifton. In this Nottinghamshire churchyard near to the river Trent, it is soft sand all the way. You won't get an easier dig than this, though, unfortunately, that often comes at a price.

I've often questioned why they attempt double-depth digs here, as the running sand is a nightmare to deal with and is unstable, even when it is shored up. The sand is so fine that on a windy day, the spoil heap can literally be blown away.

In the graveyard's older section, the majority of graves appear to be single depth, side by side. Nevertheless, it's the old story: once a gravedigger has managed to reach the mandatory six feet, it is then deemed possible to do, and so it quickly becomes the norm.

When working in this churchyard, it pays to allow extra time and to shore up your dig, as the land can seldom support itself. In recent weeks the weather had been dry, and as I hadn't foreseen the weather changing so dramatically, I neglected to follow my own advice.

Come the morning, I was dreading going back to the churchyard. I was expecting the worst.

I slid back the walk-boards. I was amazed to find that the grave was still standing – but not for long.

As the skies darkened, more heavy rain began to fall. It was torrential.

I'd just finished placing the green sheets when I heard an almighty thud. I knew what had occurred: it had caved in. Painstakingly, I cleared it out as quickly as I could, but the soft sand kept tumbling back in.

I informed the undertaker, expressing my concerns regarding the grave standing for any length of time. I was worried that if the other side caved in while they were in church, it could potentially be a problem.

He was in agreement and declared that due to the severity of the collapse, he'd advise the vicar that it might be better to hold the interment before having the church service. This was the sensible thing to do.

However, the vicar said, 'No, we will proceed as normal.'

In the pouring rain I stood by the grave, willing the long church service to end. I moved away only as the vicar and the mourners gathered at the graveside. Instead of quickly lowering in the coffin, the vicar spent another lengthy few minutes speaking, and then, just as the bearers began to lower, the grave collapsed on the opposite side. At this point, there was nothing anyone could do.

The grave was now shallow, and, to make things worse, the coffin had been pushed by the force of the collapse and was resting on its side.

I knew that once everyone had moved away, I could rectify this by removing spoil from around the coffin, thus allowing it to rest level. Unfortunately, I could not enter the grave, as two family members had requested to help me backfill, so it would have been wrong for me to do so.

If the vicar had only taken our advice, this catastrophe could well have been avoided. In the circumstances, having the interment first followed by the church service would have been the correct procedure.

I didn't half feel sorry for the two young lads who helped backfill, as they were only dressed in an insubstantial jacket, shirt and trousers. They were drenched!

CHAPTER 29

Newark Castle Ghost Hunt

I am a true believer in the paranormal. However, in all of my 40-plus years in my line of work, I can honestly say that I have never seen anything ghostlike or otherworldly. I have taken hundreds of photos and many minutes of video, but I've never captured anything. I have worked in eerie churchyards and cemeteries late into the evenings and early mornings. I have often found them spooky, but, somewhat disappointingly, I have yet to experience anything totally strange.

I once said this in an online message to Fred Batt of *Most Haunted* fame. He told me that I simply wasn't looking hard enough.

I think we are all capable of connecting to the other side, but alas the majority of us just don't know how to. I certainly don't pick up on anything. Maybe in my line of work it is best that I don't, as I might have frightened the life out of me.

Nevertheless, the paranormal fascinates me.

Halloween, 2017: unknown to me, my wife had purchased tickets for a five-hour ghost hunt at Newark's historic castle. I'd often mentioned that I'd like to go ghost hunting, though there was always a bit of me that refrained from doing so. This was simply due to me being a gravedigger. Daft as it may sound, I was worried that something might latch on to me and follow me home.

At 9 p.m., we met with other wannabe ghost hunters at the castle's main gate, where we were divided into groups. Throughout the evening, we took part in various paranormal activities.

Of all the events, I found table-tipping to be the most interesting and fun to do. Although I kept a keen eye on proceedings, I never saw anyone secretly move the table, nor push the glass in any way. All the same, part of me remained unconvinced, as there may have been trickery afoot.

Doing EVP (electronic voice phenomenon) work while inside the bottleneck dungeon was intriguing, but I still wasn't satisfied that we had actually caught any ghostly voices.

I was extremely apprehensive about taking part in the Ouija-board session – so much so that at the last minute, I declined, as I do believe this can summon up unwanted guests.

Some of the group reported hearing screams from the castle's oubliette: the deep pit that people were believed to have been thrown into and then forgotten about – left to die down there. Admittedly, it was eerie, but the wife and I didn't hear or pick up on anything sinister.

Towards the end of the evening, the whole group was taken to the castle's undercroft. This is a stone vaulted room, which was originally used for storing food and such like. In total darkness, we all stood in a circle. Two REM pods were placed at the centre. These are spirit communication devices. It is believed that if you ask a question, any ghosts can respond by touching the device.

While I stood there with my eyes closed, I suddenly started to feel hot, sweaty and unusually sick and dizzy. It was like I'd drunk too much beer, and it actually brought me to my knees. Out of all the folk stood in that circle, why me?

I felt a complete fool, especially when one of the paranormal team said, 'You've been affected and for your own safety you must leave the room.'

My wife escorted me outside, and once out in the fresh air, I felt OK again. My spouse, however, was in hysterics.

'I bet you're not so sceptical now, are you?' she said.

To this day, I have no idea of what occurred that evening. These days, I prefer to watch paranormal shows from the relative safety of my armchair. Just in case!

Chapter 30

Postponed Until Further Notice

November 2019 was an exceptionally wet month. Heavy rain, often torrential, left many places waterlogged, as groundwater levels reached record highs. For two months, virtually every village churchyard and cemetery I visited had a problem with rising water, and none more so than Sutton-on-Trent.

Between November 2019 and January 2020, I visited the cemetery four times. Each time, the grave had to be continually pumped out. This was not entirely unusual, as the river Trent often made an appearance here, but what *was* unusual was that on my second visit, on 17 November, I couldn't dig the grave at all.

I could see that the river Trent was slowly creeping its way across fields. In addition, the surrounding area was saturated, and water had pooled mere feet away from where I was to dig.

I cut the shape and removed the turf, but with my very first shovel, water sprung up like a fountain. I donned my wellies and continued to dig, yet it was obvious that I was not going to get any depth whatsoever.

As the interment was booked for 19 November, I promptly reported my findings. There was uncertainty about what to do, as this had never happened before. The undertaker met with the family and it was decided that the church service would take place as planned, while the burial would be rearranged.

Over the coming weeks, I returned twice more to Sutton. The water level dropped slowly and I was able to dig out a bit more. Finally, after 18 days, the rescheduled burial took place. Although I'd managed to get a passable depth, the pump was working overtime in order to keep the grave clear of water. Unfortunately, once the pump had been switched off and the coffin interred, the vicar waffled on and on so much that the water was rising – and so was the coffin. It was a mad dash to shovel soil on top in order to weigh the coffin down. I piled the grave high with soil and reinstated the turf. It looked a bit unsightly. On my next visit, however, the soil had dropped a little, and so I was able to put it right.

A few weeks later, another funeral director told me that he'd had a similar situation where the only way the gravedigger could keep the coffin in the grave was to pierce holes in it. Well, I wasn't doing that.

CHAPTER 31

Thank You, Mr Jackson

I've always found it strange how certain parts of your life just seem to happen, as if it was meant to be. For the past 41 years, I have worked as a gravedigger, and I have no idea why. I didn't actively set out to do this kind of work; if anything, it found me.

I left school in 1979. For 21 months, I worked as a trainee car paint sprayer. A job I secretly loathed. In March 1981, after being made redundant, I decided I wanted to work outside. Initially, I was given three options: the Forestry Commission, Parks and Gardens, or Newark Cemetery.

I didn't want to work for the Forestry Commission, because that meant having to go to college, which at that time I did not want to do. It was Newark Cemetery that appealed to me the most, but as I didn't fare too well at the interview, I chose instead to complete a six-month training scheme with Newark's Municipal Parks and Gardens department.

I enjoyed this, but when it came to an end there were no vacancies, and so I was pushed onto another random scheme, which I found totally unfulfilling. Nevertheless, if it hadn't been for this scheme, and for my supervisor, Mr Jackson, then the past 40 years may never have happened.

In February 1982, while working at the cricket pavilion in Gunthorpe, Nottinghamshire, Mr Jackson's team of six was set the task of digging a trench, for a new water pipe, from the pavilion to the pitch. The trench extended quite a distance. It had to be a spade's width wide and dug to a depth of 30 inches.

At morning tea break, three of the team opted out, choosing instead to paint the interior of the pavilion. After lunch, there were two of us, and by the start of the following day, I was working alone.

Single-handedly, I completed the task. A thankful Mr Jackson said to me, 'You're pretty good at this type of work. I know a gravedigger that lives in the next village to me. I'll have a word. If I can get you some Saturday work, would you be interested?'

I jumped at the chance.

That gravedigger was Michael North. He would become a good friend – although I wouldn't meet him until some 12 years later. Sadly, within days of saying that he would put in a good word for me, Mr Jackson left his position in order to look after his ill wife. I never saw him again.

Fortunately, before he left, he updated my personal file. He highlighted the fact that I was interested in cemetery work. He stipulated that before my current course finished, I was to be encouraged to write letters to local councils and funeral directors, enquiring about possible vacancies.

I only wrote the one letter, but it led to a permanent job at Newark Cemetery.

Many years later, I told my story to Michael North. He had indeed known Mr Jackson. He himself had dug Mr Jackson's grave, which can be found in East Stoke churchyard.

I knew Mr North for over 25 years. When he retired from gravedigging in 2004, I took on his work. He was a lovely man and respected by many. I never got the chance to dig alongside him, but when he died in April 2018 I had the honour of digging his grave.

So, thank you, Mr Jackson. If it hadn't been for you, then the last 41 years may never have happened.

CHAPTER 32

It's Time to Share the Workload

On Friday 20 December 2019, while working in the churchyard at Staunton in the Vale, Nottinghamshire, I came within a spade's width of quitting the job I'd always enjoyed doing.

In the six weeks leading up to this, I had endured nothing but wind, rain and waterlogged land. My workload had been gruelling, and for the first time ever, I was feeling demoralised and downtrodden. I was at breaking point.

My wife had passed in July of that year. I was exhausted. I had anxiety issues that later resulted in me having a panic attack, which frightened the life out of me to the point where I thought I was going to die.

The job at Staunton was problematic from start to finish. It was one of those winter days where it rained heavily, all day, and never got light.

I arrived at the church to find that the grave had completely filled with water.

The more I pumped it clear, the quicker it came back in. For three hours I tolerated torrential rain as I persevered in an attempt to keep the grave empty of water. It was an unachievable task, but one that had to be done.

The vicar assured me that the church service would last for 40 minutes, but it went on for over an hour. Twenty minutes after the committal, the family were still stood by the grave, by which time it was practically dark.

Hand-balling in sopping wet stone and clay while racing against fading daylight is no mean feat, and I'd had enough. I was wet, cold and fed up.

You can't work safely in the dark. As soon as I'd re-placed the last sod of turf, I was in the van and gone. I just left everything. The walk-boards, the green sheets, the groundsheet. I discarded the lot. And I didn't return to collect my equipment until the following Monday.

Reflecting over the weekend, I knew that I couldn't continue working alone. I needed help. I had been looking for someone for quite some time. Colleagues had come and gone. None had showed any real commitment to the job, as they found it physically too demanding.

To this day, I'm certain that one particular undertaker realised I was teetering on the edge, and struggling. He was right.

For nine years, I had pretty much toiled alone, and I'd been more than happy to do so. But I realised that now was the time to lighten the load.

Additionally, I had become aware that over the past few years, the graves I was digging were often 50 per cent bigger than they used to be. The old-style, traditional coffin with fixed handles was frequently being replaced by larger wicker, willow, seagrass, banana leaf and cardboard (or eco-board) coffins. This meant extra digging in areas that were simply not designed for such big coffins.

One Saturday in February 2020, while preparing a grave in the churchyard at Ragnall, I met David Longden. I had arranged to meet someone else, but Dave, who is related to this other chap, came in his place. From first setting eyes on him, I had a feeling that we'd get along; he was wearing a T-shirt of the American punk band the Misfits.

We chatted briefly about the job and what it entails, and I arranged for him to meet me two days later back at Ragnall, where he assisted me with a backfill.

Fast forward three years, and Dave (aka Dave the Grave) has now helped me prepare over 250 graves. It's safe to say that without Dave's assistance, I may not have completed 41 years in the business. I'm also happy that Dave has declared that he's more than willing to continue with the somewhat endangered craft of hand-digging a grave.

Good man, and good luck!

CHAPTER 33

Don't Go to Syerston

I was on my way to Syerston village, Nottinghamshire, and well past the point of no return, when I received a telephone call, informing me that I shouldn't bother going to Syerston for the day's 11 a.m. burial as it had been cancelled.

Within a matter of minutes, I arrived at the church. As luck would have it, I was met by a man who asked, 'Are you the gravedigger?'

'Yes,' I replied, 'I've just been told there's a problem with the grave's position and the plot is not going to be used.'

'That's right,' he confirmed. 'The service is going ahead at 11 a.m., but the burial has been postponed. I'm afraid you're going to have to backfill the empty grave and re-dig another at a later date.'

Dave and I had prepared this grave on 10 July, five days prior to the funeral. While digging, we had been visited by two people, one of whom said, 'I'm surprised it's being dug there. I would have thought it would have been sited near to other family members.'

'I hope it's in the right place,' I joked, 'because I wouldn't want to have to dig it twice.'

It was only on the night prior to the burial that the mistake had been discovered by the family themselves. After consultation with the vicar and undertaker, it was decided, a mere two hours before the funeral service, that the interment would be rescheduled.

The time now was 9.45 a.m. On that day, I had three full burials and two interments of ashes in five different villages.

When working out my day, I'd arranged for Dave to cover a burial at Carlton-on-Trent, which was also at 11 a.m. He was then going to join me for a 2 p.m. burial at Shelton.

As I could do nothing at Syerston, I went and dressed the grave in nearby Shelton. From there, I shot across to Balderton to prepare a burial of ashes, also for 2 p.m.

The second burial of ashes, in Norwell, was at 2.30 p.m. This I had prepared the day before, and as luck would have it, the churchwarden kindly offered to backfill this for me, thus saving me an extra journey.

From Balderton, I rushed back to Syerston, where I sat and waited for the church service to finish. Once the mourners had dispersed, I backfilled the unused plot.

Thirteen days later, Dave and I returned to dig a second grave. At least this time it was in the right place.

CHAPTER 34

Who Put That There?

In August 2022, after completing six exhausting summer digs in a row in heat surpassing 35 degrees, I said to Dave, 'It'll be nice to end the week with an extremely easy two-hour reopen dig.'

The prospect of this came as quite a relief. Only a few days earlier, we'd toiled, sweltering, to the point of collapse, while preparing a grave in the village of Screveton. I've endured some hot summers, but in all my years I had never worked in heat like that, and I hope never to again.

The humidity was draining, the sun relentless and the heat stifling. It was not the best weather to be hand-digging graves.

Feeling positive that it was the last job of the week, we made our way to North Collingham churchyard. Situated in the shade, under the trees and out of the mid-afternoon sun, we cheerfully got stuck into an easy, sand-based dig.

But what should have been a straightforward job quickly became yet another problematic and time-consuming challenge. At a depth of about 18 inches, both Dave and I realised we were repeatedly hitting upon something solid.

What we eventually unearthed was a three-feet-wide by two-feet-deep block of concrete with steel pins running through it, which had been purposely fixed directly across the grave we were reopening. This was not supposed to be there.

Eventually, the undertaker and two churchwardens arrived to assess the situation. The deceased's daughter was also called so that she could see first-hand what had been uncovered.

It transpired that this concrete block had been securely positioned in order to underpin the churchyard's surrounding wall.

The question was, who would let this happen knowing that at some point in time this grave would need to be reopened? Whoever had carried out the work had obviously not been informed, and so was none the wiser.

After what seemed ages of just standing around staring, evaluating the job, I said, 'The best thing would be to cut off the steel pins flush to the concrete block, and dig the grave just off-centre to the original grave. This way I can get the depth I need.'

I was aware that the coffin was a bulky wicker basket. That meant that the grave would partially encroach on the adjoining grave, which would also, at some point, need reopening. But that was a problem for another day.

Thankfully, all were in agreement, and with that we wasted no time in continuing with the dig.

After the funeral, I was thanked by the family for getting around the problem, thus allowing the burial to take place. I on the other hand would like to thank the man who came and cut the steel pins for us. I have no idea who you were, but thank you!

CHAPTER 35

The Covid Pandemic

People often ask me about the pandemic outbreak of 2020. 'Ooh, I bet you were busy,' they say.

To be honest, between the start of lockdown in March 2020 and the end of December 2022 – 30 months in total – I dug 226 full graves, with an additional 208 burials of cremated remains. I did not experience any particular rise. My workload remained average.

Furthermore, throughout the pandemic I wasn't instructed or advised to follow any particular guidelines or indeed told to use any specific PPE. The only precautionary measure I took was to spray the webbings used for lowering the coffin, as well as the putlogs, with disinfectant or Jeyes Fluid, and when handling any floral tributes, of which there weren't many, we wore gloves.

All burials were limited in terms of the number of attendees, and all were shortened graveside services. Apart from at the onset of the pandemic, I wasn't specifically notified as to whether the deceased had died from Covid or not. Truth is, we didn't need to be informed, as there was little danger for us.

My first confirmed Covid burial was on 9 April 2020. There were just three family members in attendance.

At times it was impossible for Dave and me to keep two metres apart, as we often had to work in close proximity, though we did travel between jobs separately. We both found it near impossible to wear face masks when digging, as it restricted our breathing and simply got in our way.

Additionally, although somewhat distrustfully I may add, we both followed protocol and had our Covid-19 vaccinations.

What a strange time it was.

Now, three years on, I'm the only person within my family who hasn't contracted Covid. Maybe that has been because I live alone, and except for fetching supplies, I didn't mix or go out anywhere, thus keeping myself to myself. In doing that, I may just have been extremely lucky.

I once read an article about a gravedigger in London during the great plague of 1348–49. Although he handled and buried hundreds of plague victims, he never caught the plague. He worked continuously and lived and slept in a shed. Relatives of the dead left him food and wine at the cemetery gates.

I've frequently wondered what would have happened if either Dave or I had caught Covid and been forced into isolation. Who would have dug the graves?

This was never discussed.

CHAPTER 36

Graveyard Antics

Car keys

The most bizarre request I have ever had from an undertaker has to be: 'Have you got a fishing rod in your van?'

During a burial at Newark Cemetery, a lady had accidentally dropped her car keys into the grave, and they had landed on top of the coffin. The lady was highly embarrassed. Obviously, she was keen to retrieve them, and so the undertaker asked me if I had anything he could use.

My first thought was to grab my ladder and climb down into the grave. However, as immediate family members were still present, this was deemed to be a last-resort option.

By chance, I happened to have a metal fencing stake which had a small hook on the end. I could only watch as the undertaker and two of his bearers precariously knelt on the walk-boards, reaching down to grip hold of the keys.

After a few failed attempts and a lot of clowning about, they eventually pulled it off.

Firework

I was once busy bottoming out a double-depth grave when all of a sudden it went dark. The walk-boards above me had been pulled closed, and behind me I could hear a loud fizzing noise. I realised what it was, but before I could react, there was an enormous bang.

My workmate thought it would be a great idea to drop a firework – a banger – into the bottom of the grave. In such an enclosed space, the deafening boom made my legs buckle and my ears throb. My colleague thought it was hilarious, but I was left unable to hear, albeit temporarily.

Have a sniff

I never did get my workmate back for the above prank, though two lads from the Commonwealth War Graves Commission certainly did. They had arrived to clean the headstones, and as they were preparing to do so, my colleague and I stopped for a chat.

One of them said to my colleague, 'Here, come and have a sniff at this. You'll like it. When I remove the lid, inhale a deep breath and then stand back.'

Foolishly, my workmate did as he was asked. Almost immediately, he fell backwards, collapsing onto the grass.

The other guy shouted to his mate, 'Bloody hell, you idiot, you've killed him!'

After a few seconds, my colleague staggered to his feet. He was in a really bad way. He was drooling, his eyes were bright red, his nose was running and his throat was on fire. Fortunately, they were able to deal with his symptoms, and within a few minutes he was back in the land of the living, though he had a banging headache.

My colleague had only inhaled some extremely potent, industrial-strength ammonia.

Snow joke

With the night's heavy snowfall, it was a foregone conclusion that at some point during the day, there would be a free-for-all snowball fight. What was unfair was that when you were six feet underground, you had no means of fighting back. Pinned down by two of my colleagues, I could do nothing but cower in the corner of the grave as snowball after snowball showered down upon me.

The snowball fight then quickly spread as passing schoolkids decided to take us all on.

Unfortunately for him, a passing policeman got caught up in the snowball frenzy, and everyone focused their aim on him. One snowball struck him directly on his helmet and another hit him firmly between the shoulder blades.

The kids ran off in various directions, a colleague disappeared behind a tree, and my other colleague and I quickly climbed down and hid in the grave.

The policeman had no idea who the culprit was, though he did shout across to us, 'Grow up, lads,' before continuing on his way.

Pete's tree

I'd just shut off my mower and was taking a break under the shade of a tree when my boss appeared.

'Where's Pete?' he asked. 'He's supposed to be cutting grass, but I can't find him anywhere.'

I didn't have the heart to tell him that Pete was seated in the tree, smiling and pulling faces, directly above where our boss was standing.

It was as much as I could do not to laugh, as that most certainly would have revealed his whereabouts.

Throughout the summer of 1987, Pete could often be found resting in what became known as Pete's tree, and our boss never cottoned on.

Married in work time?

It was bad enough that I could never take a lengthy holiday, but while I was contracted to the council, I had to appeal to councillors in order to have a single day off to get married.

Although they eventually granted me permission, they were quick to point out that I was contracted to provide a service, and therefore I had to provide adequate cover. Unfortunately, my brother was my sole assistant at the time, and so they wrongly assumed that he would be on hand to cover the day.

It was ridiculous. I contacted the local funeral director myself and explained the situation, and they were more than happy to book no funerals for that day.

No, we did not have a honeymoon. That was out of the question.

Mobile phone

I was in the process of backfilling a burial when the funeral director appeared and said, 'You've not heard a mobile phone ringing, have you?'

He went on to explain that the deceased had requested that his mobile phone be buried with him.

That was fine; however, the funeral director confessed that he had forgotten to remove the battery.

Just imagine if someone had tried calling the deceased while he was being transported in the back of the hearse, during the service or as he was being laid to rest.

Mind you, if it had rung and he'd answered it, then we really would've panicked.

Langford Neil

I first met Neil Grebbie, or Langford Neil as I call him, at Langford Church on 6 May 2005. I was preparing a grave and he was cutting the grass. We became friends, and 11 years later, on 8 September 2016, he asked me if he could help prepare a grave for a friend of his at Holme Church.

Seven years later and he has now assisted me locally with about 40 digs. He's 76 this year. His apprenticeship is nearing its end (ha ha).

It amazes me how someone of his age is still willing to do some manual toil, especially when today's youth will not even consider it. Well done, Neil, and thank you for all your help.

I can safely say that I will not be digging at his age.

Blue cordial

'I'm thirsty,' said my young trainee colleague one day. 'I've drunk all the pop I brought with me. Is there a shop nearby?'

'There's no shop in this village,' I informed him, 'but if you look in my van, under the passenger seat you'll find some made-up cordial. You can have that.'

'Ooh, thanks,' he said, and off he went to fetch it.

On his return, he said, 'What is that blue pop? It tastes disgusting. It's made my throat feel funny.'

I looked at him. 'What blue pop? There's a bottle of orange squash, but nothing blue.'

It was then that the penny dropped.

I laughed out loud. 'You didn't drink that, did you? Because that is diluted window wash for the van.'

'Oh,' he said. 'I did have a couple of swigs, but it was horrible, so I spat it out.'

I didn't half laugh.

Cave-ins

During the 1970s and early 1980s, preparing graves in the village of Balderton often came at a price. Apparently, when British Gypsum used to blast rock in the nearby quarry, the ground would vibrate and shake, and if you happened to be digging a grave, then the mixture of soft sand and gravel would invariably cave in.

It was the same in the village of South Muskham, Nottinghamshire. The churchyard is close to the main London to Glasgow railway line. Often, the old steam trains and later the heavy diesels would slowly chug by, vibrating the earth and causing it to cave in. How annoying!

A disgruntled son

As the mourners filed out of the churchyard, one young man tapped on my van window.

'Are you the gravedigger?' he asked.

'Yes,' I replied.

'You've buried both my mother and father within three weeks of each other,' he said. 'Enjoy your summer holiday, on me.'

I had no words.

CHAPTER 37

A 34-Year Secret

After 34 years I believe I can finally reveal the somewhat secretive story behind the mysterious case of the missing antique.

Although it has been in my possession for the past three decades, I must make it known that I was completely innocent in the obtaining of this historic item. It was simply dumped on me.

I always said that one day I would return it to its rightful owner, and that time is now.

It all began in 1989 with the annual invite to Newark Town Hall for a Christmas drink with the mayor. No staff member really wanted to attend, as the event had been arranged over our lunch break. Furthermore, I wasn't keen because I'd volunteered to cover a late burial. Nevertheless, pressure from our acting superintendent and whispers of disciplinary action for non-attendees meant that we had no choice but to be present.

Over the years, previous functions had been solemn, dreary affairs, with little atmosphere, warm beer, stale sausage rolls and bland mince pies. Usually, we were served up with whatever was left over from the previous night's festivities.

The recently appointed mayor, however, unlike his predecessors, was regarded for his generosity, and it was well known that he enjoyed a drink. Our host was quick to drop his mayoral guise and openly joined in, and, yes, the food was enjoyable and the beer and shorts flowed freely. Much too freely.

Our allocated one-hour slot soon spread to two, and it was only the intervention of our boss, reminding us of our pending funeral, that finally moved us on.

It's safe to say that some staff members had taken it a bit far and were very, very drunk. As we made our way out of the town hall, many decorative plants were removed from their pots and turned upside down. The mayor's Christmas tree was toppled over, and bottles of vodka, whiskey and rum were half-inched from the mayor's private parlour. It was carnage!

In fear of missing the burial, I and three others crammed into the cab of Newark's tiny street-sweeping machine, named 'Big Boris'. How on earth we all got in the two-seater vehicle and got safely back to the cemetery, I'll never know.

With the grave complete and the end of our shift nearing, I retired with a colleague to the warmth of the staff messroom. The place was buzzing with Christmas cheer, and on the table was an array of booty that had been pocketed from our earlier trip to the town hall.

It was at that precise moment that someone yelled, 'The boss is coming,' and with just seconds to spare before his arrival, everything on the table was cleared and the room fell quiet. Our boss proceeded to give us a severe telling-off. Even though at this point he had no idea of the mess that some of us had left behind, he was not a happy man.

Unknown to me, two of the pilfered items had been slipped into the pockets of my work coat. I only found this out as I was leaving to go home. I didn't pay too much attention to it, but as I couldn't leave the coat hanging around the messroom, I placed it in my locker.

On returning to work in the new year, our boss announced to us all that a key item had gone missing from the town hall. Apparently, it had significant historic value for the town, and its whereabouts were sought. Town councillors had implemented a seven-day amnesty during which the item could be returned.

My colleagues who had acquired it were quick to distance themselves, stating, 'It was in your pocket. You deal with it.'

Three days later, I found out that a colleague had sneakily reported that the item was in one of our lockers. That morning, at tea break, the town clerk and his assistant arrived to do an impromptu locker search.

It could have been extremely embarrassing, and I would have been left taking one for the team, but fortunately I had removed the item and taken it home.

So, what was all the fuss about?

The object in question was a hammer and gavel. It was deemed to be extremely old and had been used by various visiting dignitaries to the town.

It was believed to have been used during the civil war siege of Newark during the late 1640s.

It was understood that King Charles I had used it, while in Newark, just three months prior to his execution.

For over 30 years, it has been safely stashed in the bottom of a chest of drawers. I think it's finally time for it to be returned from whence it came.

The End

Milton Keynes UK
Ingram Content Group UK Ltd.
UKHW010639310823
427815UK00001B/2